The UNITED STATES PRESIDENTS

Richard

NIXON

Tamara L. Britton

Big Buddy Books

An Imprint of Abdo Publishing
abdopublishing.com

abdopublishing.com

Published by Abdo Publishing, a division of ABDO, PO Box 398166, Minneapolis, Minnesota 55439.
Copyright © 2017 by Abdo Consulting Group, Inc. International copyrights reserved in all countries. No part of this book may be reproduced in any form without written permission from the publisher. Big Buddy Books™ is a trademark and logo of Abdo Publishing.

Printed in the United States of America, North Mankato, Minnesota
062016
092016

THIS BOOK CONTAINS RECYCLED MATERIALS

Design: Sarah DeYoung, Mighty Media, Inc.
Production: Mighty Media, Inc.
Editor: Lauren Kukla
Cover Photograph: Getty Images
Interior Photographs: AP Images (pp. 7, 9, 11, 17, 19, 21, 23, 27, 29); Corbis (pp. 5, 6, 13, 15);
    iStockphoto (p. 25)

Cataloging-in-Publication Data

Names: Britton, Tamara L., author.
Title: Richard Nixon / by Tamara L. Britton.
Description: Minneapolis, MN : Abdo Publishing, [2017] | Series: United States
    presidents | Includes bibliographical references and index.
Identifiers: LCCN 2015957555 | ISBN 9781680781106 (lib. bdg.) |
    ISBN 9781680775303 (ebook)
Subjects: LCSH: Nixon, Richard M. (Richard Milhous), 1913-1994--Juvenile
    literature. | Presidents--United States--Biography--Juvenile literature. |
    United States--Politics and government--1969-1974--Juvenile literature.
Classification: DDC 973.924/092 [B]--dc23
LC record available at http://lccn.loc.gov/2015957555

Contents

Richard Nixon

In 1969, Richard Nixon became the thirty-seventh president of the United States. It was a great accomplishment. Nixon had come from a poor family. He worked hard to earn success.

As president, Nixon worked toward world peace. He passed laws to improve life for Americans. However, Nixon made some bad decisions during his first term. As a result, Nixon became the first US president to **resign** from office.

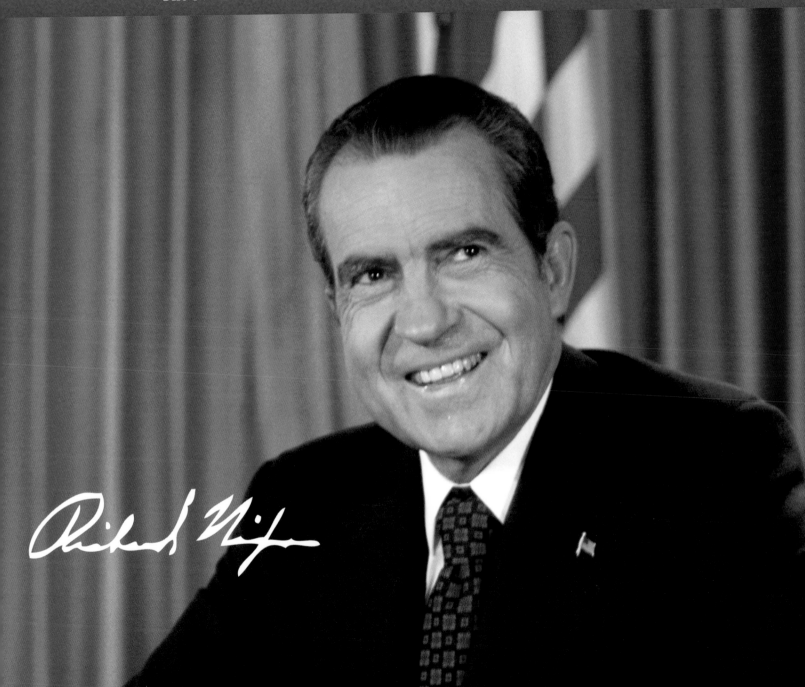

Timeline

1913

On January 9, Richard Milhous Nixon was born in Yorba Linda, California.

1960

Nixon lost the presidential election to John F. Kennedy on November 8.

1952

Nixon was elected vice president under Dwight D. Eisenhower on November 4.

1969

On January 20, Nixon became the thirty-seventh US president.

1972

Burglars broke into a **Democratic** office at the Watergate Hotel on June 17. Nixon was reelected on November 7.

1973

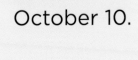

Vice President Spiro T. Agnew **resigned** on October 10.

1974

Nixon resigned on August 9. Vice President Gerald Ford became president.

1994

Richard Nixon died on April 22.

Early Years

Richard Milhous Nixon was born in Yorba Linda, California, on January 9, 1913. His parents were Francis and Hannah Nixon. Francis owned a gas station and grocery store. Richard and his four brothers worked there after school.

★ FAST FACTS ★

Born: January 9, 1913

Wife: Thelma Catherine Patricia "Pat" Ryan (1912–1993)

Children: two

Political Party: Republican

Age at Inauguration: 56

Years Served: 1969–1974

Vice Presidents: Spiro T. Agnew, Gerald Ford

Died: April 22, 1994, age 81

Richard (*far right*) and his family

Student Leader

In 1930, Richard entered Whittier College in California. There, he was elected class president. In 1934, he finished second in his class.

Richard's success earned him a **scholarship**. He entered Duke University School of Law in Durham, North Carolina. At Duke, Richard was known for his leadership.

After finishing law school in 1937, Richard returned to Whittier, California. There, he joined the law firm of Wingert and Bewley. Richard soon became a **partner**.

At Whittier, Richard played on the football team. At first, he wasn't a great player. But he became better with practice.

Family Man

In 1940, Nixon married Thelma Catherine Patricia Ryan. She went by the name Pat. They went on to have two daughters.

Meanwhile, **World War II** had started in 1939. In 1942, Nixon joined the US Navy. After the war ended, the Nixons moved to Maryland.

In 1945, a Whittier **political** group asked Nixon to run for Congress. He and his family returned to California to campaign. In November 1946, Nixon won a seat in the US House of **Representatives**.

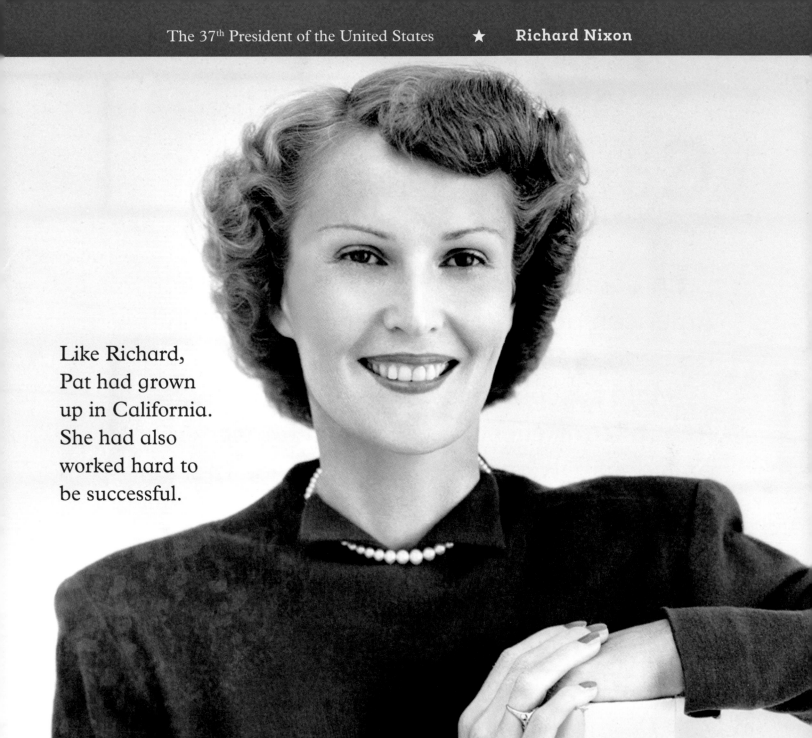

Like Richard, Pat had grown up in California. She had also worked hard to be successful.

Congressman

In Congress, Nixon worked to serve the American people. He then ran for a seat in the US Senate. Nixon easily won the election.

More success followed. In 1952, the **Republicans** chose Nixon to run for vice president. Dwight D. Eisenhower was their presidential **candidate**.

But a few days later, a newspaper printed a story about Nixon. It said that he took money and gifts in return for **political** favors. Some Republicans wanted to remove Nixon as the vice presidential candidate.

Eisenhower (*left*) and Nixon on the campaign trail

In September 1952, Nixon gave a speech on TV. In it, he claimed he had never used the money for himself. And, no one got **political** favors in return for money or gifts.

Nixon also said someone had given him a cocker spaniel. His daughter Tricia had named the dog Checkers. Nixon said his family was going to keep Checkers.

Nixon told Americans he did not want to quit running for vice president. But he would step down if they felt he should. The speech was a success. Nixon stayed in the running. Eisenhower and Nixon won the election!

Nixon's 1952 speech became known as the Checkers speech.

Vice President

Nixon was an active vice president. He went to many **cabinet** meetings. He traveled the world giving speeches. He even took over presidential duties when Eisenhower was ill.

In 1960, the **Republican** Party chose Nixon to run for president. He ran against **Democrat** John F. Kennedy. The two men **debated** on TV.

Nixon was a strong debater. But, he had been sick with the flu. So, he did not look good. Kennedy looked young and strong.

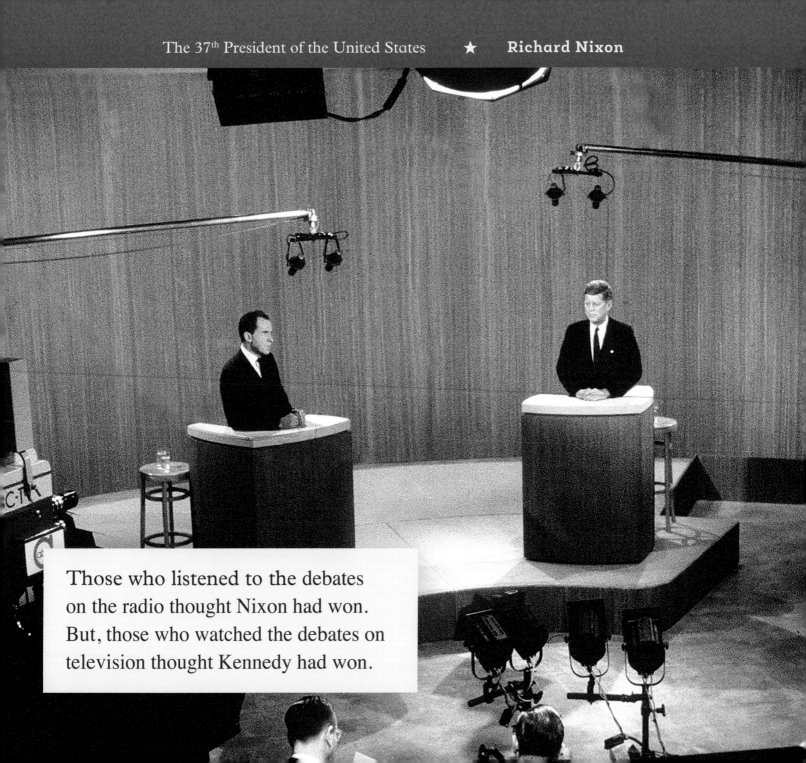

Those who listened to the debates on the radio thought Nixon had won. But, those who watched the debates on television thought Kennedy had won.

On November 8, 1960, Kennedy beat Nixon. It was one of the closest elections in US history. It was also the first time Nixon lost an election.

Nixon returned to California. Two years later, he ran for governor. But, he lost that election too. Nixon's work in **politics** seemed to be over.

The Nixons then moved to New York. There, Nixon worked as a **lawyer**. But already, he was thinking about his future in politics.

★ DID YOU KNOW? ★

The 1960 presidential election was not the first time Richard Nixon and John F. Kennedy **debated**. In April 1947, the two congressmen debated a labor act in McKeesport, Pennsylvania.

Almost 69 million people voted in the 1960 presidential election. This gave it the highest voter turnout of the 1900s.

President Nixon

Nixon did not run for president in 1964. Instead, he campaigned for **Republican** Barry Goldwater. However, Goldwater lost the election.

Nixon continued to campaign for other **politicians**. In 1966, he visited 35 states. Nixon's hard work helped many Republicans win elections that year.

In 1968, the Republicans picked Nixon to run for president. On November 5, he beat Hubert H. Humphrey. On January 20, 1969, Nixon officially became president.

PRESIDENT NIXON'S CABINET

First Term
January 20, 1969–January 20, 1973

- ★ **STATE:** William P. Rogers
- ★ **TREASURY:** David M. Kennedy,
  John B. Connally Jr. (from February 11, 1971),
  George P. Shultz (from June 12, 1972)
- ★ **DEFENSE:** Melvin R. Laird
- ★ **ATTORNEY GENERAL:** John N. Mitchell,
  Richard G. Kleindienst (from June 12, 1972)
- ★ **INTERIOR:** Walter J. Hickel,
  Rogers C.B. Morton (from January 29, 1971)
- ★ **AGRICULTURE:** Clifford M. Hardin,
  Earl L. Butz (from December 2, 1971)
- ★ **COMMERCE:** Maurice H. Stans,
  Peter G. Peterson (from February 21, 1972)
- ★ **LABOR:** George P. Shultz,
  James D. Hodgson (from July 2, 1970)
- ★ **HEALTH, EDUCATION, AND WELFARE:**
  Robert H. Finch,
  Elliot L. Richardson (from June 24, 1970)
- ★ **HOUSING AND URBAN DEVELOPMENT:**
  George W. Romney
- ★ **TRANSPORTATION:** John A. Volpe

Second Term
January 20, 1973–August 9, 1974

- ★ **STATE:** William P. Rogers,
  Henry A. Kissinger (from September 22, 1973)
- ★ **TREASURY:** George P. Shultz,
  William E. Simon (from May 8, 1974)
- ★ **DEFENSE:** Elliot L. Richardson,
  James R. Schlesinger (from July 2, 1973)
- ★ **ATTORNEY GENERAL:** Richard G. Kleindienst,
  Elliot L. Richardson (from May 25, 1973),
  William B. Saxbe (from January 4, 1974)
- ★ **INTERIOR:** Rogers C.B. Morton
- ★ **AGRICULTURE:** Earl L. Butz
- ★ **COMMERCE:** Frederick B. Dent
- ★ **LABOR:** Peter J. Brennan
- ★ **HEALTH, EDUCATION, AND WELFARE:**
  Caspar W. Weinberger
- ★ **HOUSING AND URBAN DEVELOPMENT:**
  James T. Lynn
- ★ **TRANSPORTATION:** Claude S. Brinegar

Nixon (*right*) and Vice President Spiro T. Agnew

23

Peacemaker

During Nixon's presidency, the United States took part in the **Vietnam War** and other wars. Nixon promised he would work for world peace. To this end, he met with many world leaders.

At home, Nixon cut government spending. He helped keep the cost of products from increasing. On November 7, 1972, Nixon easily won reelection.

★ SUPREME COURT ★ APPOINTMENTS

Warren E. Burger: 1969

Harry A. Blackmun: 1970

Lewis F. Powell Jr.: 1972

William H. Rehnquist: 1972

More than
58,000
Americans
died in the
Vietnam War.

A Tragic Ending

Despite Nixon's popularity, a **scandal** soon overshadowed his success. On June 17, 1972, burglars were caught breaking into an office in the Watergate Hotel building in Washington, DC. Some **Republicans** had hired them to steal **information** from the **Democrats**.

Nixon knew about the break-in. He also tried to cover it up. Congress wanted to **impeach** Nixon for his actions. So, Nixon **resigned** on August 9, 1974. Vice President Gerald Ford became president.

Ford (*shown*) had become vice president when Spiro T. Agnew resigned as vice president on October 10, 1973.

Statesman

After Nixon left the White House, he worked hard to win back America's respect. He wrote books on **politics** and world peace. Nixon also gave advice to US presidents.

Pat Nixon died on June 22, 1993. Less than one year later, Richard Nixon had a **stroke**. He died from it on April 22, 1994, in New York City.

Many Americans only remember Nixon for the Watergate **scandal**. But as president, he helped improve the lives of Americans. Richard Nixon worked to bring peace to the world.

Left to right: Presidents Ronald Reagan, Richard Nixon, George H.W. Bush, and Gerald Ford at the Richard Nixon Library & Birthplace in Yorba Linda

Office of the President

Branches of Government

The US government has three branches. They are the executive, legislative, and judicial branches. Each branch has some power over the others. This is called a system of checks and balances.

★ Executive Branch

The executive branch enforces laws. It is made up of the president, the vice president, and the president's cabinet. The president represents the United States around the world. He or she also signs bills into law and leads the military.

★ Legislative Branch

The legislative branch makes laws, maintains the military, and regulates trade. It also has the power to declare war. This branch includes the Senate and the House of Representatives. Together, these two houses form Congress.

★ Judicial Branch

The judicial branch interprets laws. It is made up of district courts, courts of appeals, and the Supreme Court. District courts try cases. Sometimes people disagree with a trial's outcome. Then he or she may appeal. If a court of appeals supports the ruling, a person may appeal to the Supreme Court.

Qualifications for Office

To be president, a candidate must be at least 35 years old. The person must be a natural-born US citizen. He or she must also have lived in the United States for at least 14 years.

Electoral College

The US presidential election is an indirect election. Voters from each state choose electors. These electors represent their state in the Electoral College. Each elector has one electoral vote. Electors cast their vote for the candidate with the highest number of votes from people in their state. A candidate must receive the majority of Electoral College votes to win.

Term of Office

Each president may be elected to two four-year terms. The presidential election is held on the Tuesday after the first Monday in November. The president is sworn in on January 20 of the following year. At that time, he or she takes the oath of office.
It states:

> I do solemnly swear (or affirm) that I will faithfully execute the office of President of the United States, and will to the best of my ability, preserve, protect and defend the Constitution of the United States.

31

Line of Succession

The Presidential Succession Act of 1947 states who becomes president if the president cannot serve. The vice president is first in the line. Next are the Speaker of the House and the President Pro Tempore of the Senate. It may happen that none of these individuals is able to serve. Then the office falls to the president's cabinet members. They would take office in the order in which each department was created:

Secretary of State

Secretary of the Treasury

Secretary of Defense

Attorney General

Secretary of the Interior

Secretary of Agriculture

Secretary of Commerce

Secretary of Labor

Secretary of Health and Human Services

Secretary of Housing and Urban Development

Secretary of Transportation

Secretary of Energy

Secretary of Education

Secretary of Veterans Affairs

Secretary of Homeland Security

Benefits

★ While in office, the president receives a salary. It is $400,000 per year. He or she lives in the White House. The president also has 24-hour Secret Service protection.

★ The president may travel on a Boeing 747 jet. This special jet is called Air Force One. It can hold 70 passengers. It has kitchens, a dining room, sleeping areas, and more. Air Force One can fly halfway around the world before needing to refuel. It can even refuel in flight!

★ When the president travels by car, he or she uses Cadillac One. It is a Cadillac Deville that has been modified. The car has heavy armor and communications systems. The president may even take Cadillac One along when visiting other countries.

★ The president also travels on a helicopter. It is called Marine One. It may also be taken along when the president visits other countries.

★ Sometimes the president needs to get away with family and friends. Camp David is the official presidential retreat. It is located in Maryland. The US Navy maintains the retreat. The US Marine Corps keeps it secure. The camp offers swimming, tennis, golf, and hiking.

★ When the president leaves office, he or she receives lifetime Secret Service protection. He or she also receives a yearly pension of $203,700. The former president also receives money for office space, supplies, and staff.

PRESIDENTS AND THEIR TERMS

PRESIDENT	PARTY	TOOK OFFICE	LEFT OFFICE	TERMS SERVED	VICE PRESIDENT
George Washington	None	April 30, 1789	March 4, 1797	Two	John Adams
John Adams	Federalist	March 4, 1797	March 4, 1801	One	Thomas Jefferson
Thomas Jefferson	Democratic-Republican	March 4, 1801	March 4, 1809	Two	Aaron Burr, George Clinton
James Madison	Democratic-Republican	March 4, 1809	March 4, 1817	Two	George Clinton, Elbridge Gerry
James Monroe	Democratic-Republican	March 4, 1817	March 4, 1825	Two	Daniel D. Tompkins
John Quincy Adams	Democratic-Republican	March 4, 1825	March 4, 1829	One	John C. Calhoun
Andrew Jackson	Democrat	March 4, 1829	March 4, 1837	Two	John C. Calhoun, Martin Van Buren
Martin Van Buren	Democrat	March 4, 1837	March 4, 1841	One	Richard M. Johnson
William H. Harrison	Whig	March 4, 1841	April 4, 1841	Died During First Term	John Tyler
John Tyler	Whig	April 6, 1841	March 4, 1845	Completed Harrison's Term	Office Vacant
James K. Polk	Democrat	March 4, 1845	March 4, 1849	One	George M. Dallas
Zachary Taylor	Whig	March 5, 1849	July 9, 1850	Died During First Term	Millard Fillmore

PRESIDENT	PARTY	TOOK OFFICE	LEFT OFFICE	TERMS SERVED	VICE PRESIDENT
Millard Fillmore	Whig	July 10, 1850	March 4, 1853	Completed Taylor's Term	Office Vacant
Franklin Pierce	Democrat	March 4, 1853	March 4, 1857	One	William R.D. King
James Buchanan	Democrat	March 4, 1857	March 4, 1861	One	John C. Breckinridge
Abraham Lincoln	Republican	March 4, 1861	April 15, 1865	Served One Term, Died During Second Term	Hannibal Hamlin, Andrew Johnson
Andrew Johnson	Democrat	April 15, 1865	March 4, 1869	Completed Lincoln's Second Term	Office Vacant
Ulysses S. Grant	Republican	March 4, 1869	March 4, 1877	Two	Schuyler Colfax, Henry Wilson
Rutherford B. Hayes	Republican	March 3, 1877	March 4, 1881	One	William A. Wheeler
James A. Garfield	Republican	March 4, 1881	September 19, 1881	Died During First Term	Chester Arthur
Chester Arthur	Republican	September 20, 1881	March 4, 1885	Completed Garfield's Term	Office Vacant
Grover Cleveland	Democrat	March 4, 1885	March 4, 1889	One	Thomas A. Hendricks
Benjamin Harrison	Republican	March 4, 1889	March 4, 1893	One	Levi P. Morton
Grover Cleveland	Democrat	March 4, 1893	March 4, 1897	One	Adlai E. Stevenson
William McKinley	Republican	March 4, 1897	September 14, 1901	Served One Term, Died During Second Term	Garret A. Hobart, Theodore Roosevelt

PRESIDENT	PARTY	TOOK OFFICE	LEFT OFFICE	TERMS SERVED	VICE PRESIDENT
Theodore Roosevelt	Republican	September 14, 1901	March 4, 1909	Completed McKinley's Second Term, Served One Term	Office Vacant, Charles Fairbanks
William Taft	Republican	March 4, 1909	March 4, 1913	One	James S. Sherman
Woodrow Wilson	Democrat	March 4, 1913	March 4, 1921	Two	Thomas R. Marshall
Warren G. Harding	Republican	March 4, 1921	August 2, 1923	Died During First Term	Calvin Coolidge
Calvin Coolidge	Republican	August 3, 1923	March 4, 1929	Completed Harding's Term, Served One Term	Office Vacant, Charles Dawes
Herbert Hoover	Republican	March 4, 1929	March 4, 1933	One	Charles Curtis
Franklin D. Roosevelt	Democrat	March 4, 1933	April 12, 1945	Served Three Terms, Died During Fourth Term	John Nance Garner, Henry A. Wallace, Harry S. Truman
Harry S. Truman	Democrat	April 12, 1945	January 20, 1953	Completed Roosevelt's Fourth Term, Served One Term	Office Vacant, Alben Barkley
Dwight D. Eisenhower	Republican	January 20, 1953	January 20, 1961	Two	Richard Nixon
John F. Kennedy	Democrat	January 20, 1961	November 22, 1963	Died During First Term	Lyndon B. Johnson
Lyndon B. Johnson	Democrat	November 22, 1963	January 20, 1969	Completed Kennedy's Term, Served One Term	Office Vacant, Hubert H. Humphrey
Richard Nixon	Republican	January 20, 1969	August 9, 1974	Completed First Term, Resigned During Second Term	Spiro T. Agnew, Gerald Ford

PRESIDENT	PARTY	TOOK OFFICE	LEFT OFFICE	TERMS SERVED	VICE PRESIDENT
Gerald Ford	Republican	August 9, 1974	January 20, 1977	Completed Nixon's Second Term	Nelson A. Rockefeller
Jimmy Carter	Democrat	January 20, 1977	January 20, 1981	One	Walter Mondale
Ronald Reagan	Republican	January 20, 1981	January 20, 1989	Two	George H.W. Bush
George H.W. Bush	Republican	January 20, 1989	January 20, 1993	One	Dan Quayle
Bill Clinton	Democrat	January 20, 1993	January 20, 2001	Two	Al Gore
George W. Bush	Republican	January 20, 2001	January 20, 2009	Two	Dick Cheney
Barack Obama	Democrat	January 20, 2009	January 20, 2017	Two	Joe Biden

"I have often said, what is really important in a person's life is whether they make a difference, a difference for the benefit of others." Richard Nixon

★ WRITE TO THE PRESIDENT ★

You may write to the president at:
The White House
1600 Pennsylvania Avenue NW
Washington, DC 20500

You may e-mail the president at:
comments@whitehouse.gov

Glossary

cabinet—a group of advisers chosen by the president to lead government departments.

candidate (KAN-duh-dayt)—a person who seeks a political office.

debate—to participate in a planned discussion about a question or topic, often in public.

Democrat—a member of the Democratic political party.

impeach—to charge someone for doing wrong while serving in a public office.

information (ihn-fuhr-MAY-shuhn)—knowledge obtained from learning or studying something.

lawyer (LAW-yuhr)—a person who gives people advice on laws or represents them in court.

partner—someone who is part of a group that jointly owns a business.

politics—the art or science of government. Something referring to politics is political. A person who is active in politics is a politician.

representative—someone chosen in an election to act or speak for the people who voted for him or her.

Republican—a member of the Republican political party.

resign—to give up a job, position, or office by choice.

scandal—an action that shocks people and disgraces those connected with it.

scholarship—money or aid given to help a student continue his or her studies.

stroke—a medical problem caused by lack of blood flow to the brain. Strokes are serious. They may cause brain damage or death.

Vietnam War—a war that took place between South Vietnam and North Vietnam from 1957 to 1975. The United States was involved in this war for many years.

World War II—a war fought in Europe, Asia, and Africa from 1939 to 1945.

★ WEBSITES ★

To learn more about the US Presidents, visit **booklinks.abdopublishing.com**. These links are routinely monitored and updated to provide the most current information available.

Index